8

REPORT

OF THE

[SU]RVEY OF THE NORTH AND NORTHWEST LAKES:

BY CAPT. GEORGE G. MEADE,

CORPS OF TOPOGRAPHICAL ENGINEERS,

BEING APPENDIX I

OF THE

[R]EPORT OF THE CHIEF TOPOGRAPHICAL ENGINEER,

ACCOMPANYING ANNUAL REPORT

OF THE

SECRETARY OF WAR,

1858.

WASHINGTON:

PRINTED BY LEMUEL TOWERS.

1859.

REPORT.

APPENDIX I.

UNITED STATES SURVEYING STEAMER SEARCH,
Thunder Bay, Lake Huron, October 9, 1858.

SIR: In compliance with the "General Regulations of the Army of June 1, 1857, par. 1224," I have the honor to submit the following report of the progress during the past year, of the survey of the north and northwest lakes, together with an estimate of the amount required for the further prosecution of the work.

I shall adhere, in this report, to the plan adopted in the last annual report as the one best calculated to show the character and progress of the work, of dividing it into the following heads:

I. Office work, including the reduction and engraving of charts.
II. Field operations of the current season.
III. Proposed plan of future operations, with estimates.

Office Work.

Under this head I shall confine myself to a brief summary of the work executed by the several parties in the office during the past winter and spring.

Off-shore hydrography.—The soundings made by the steamer Search in the upper portion of Saginaw bay were projected, under my direction, by Assistants J. A. Potter and Wm. Casgrain, on a scale of $\frac{1}{40000}$, making a sheet 1,152 square inches of hydrography. This sheet proves the bay to have been well sounded, and delineates very clearly the several channels and shoals. Assistants Potter and Casgrain also drew an outline chart of the lower portion of the same bay, on a scale of $\frac{1}{100000}$, for use in the field this season.

Hydrography and Topography of Shore-line.

Assistant Hearding's party, consisting of Assistants J. Forster, J. Beghein, and O. M. Chaffee, projected their work of the preceding season on the following maps:

One sheet from Point aux Barques to the light-house.....scale $\frac{1}{10000}$
Two sheets from Point aux Barques to Oak Point........scale $\frac{1}{10000}$
One sheet of the Huana Kissee marsh.................scale $\frac{1}{10000}$
One sheet of the Maumee river.......................scale $\frac{1}{10000}$
Part of the reduced chart of Maumee bay..............scale $\frac{1}{30000}$

The above sheets in all included 2,024 square inches of minute topography and hydrography.

Assistant G. W. Lamson, together with Assistants D. F. Henry and A. Lamson, projected the following maps:

Four sheets of the shore-line of Saginaw bay, extending from Towa river to near the Pinnecawling river, each on a scale of $\frac{1}{10000}$.

One sheet middle channel St. Mary's river, scale $\frac{1}{10000}$. These several sheets included 3,156 square inches of topography and dydrography.

Assistant H. C. Penny, together with Assistant H. Gillman, projected their work in two sheets on a scale of $\frac{1}{10000}$, and included in them that portion of the shore-line of Saginaw bay from Sand Point to near the Huana Kissee marsh, and containing 2,511 square inches of topography and hydrography. The areas covered by these sheets and their location can be readily seen by an inspection of the sketch of Saginaw bay, accompanying this report, where the several sheets are included in the field-work of the several parties in 1857.

Primary Triangulation.—Second Lieutenant O. M. Poe, Topographical Engineers, computed the reductions, for inclination of tubes, to the base-line measurement; also, the approximate elevation of the base-line above the sea level by the comparison of four months' barometric observations at Land Point and Blackwell's island, New York, the latter having been furnished the survey through the courtesy of Jas. Green, esq., of New York, and Dr. Sanger of the island. Having obtained the final reduction of the base, Lieutenant Poe discussed and reduced the angles observed, and computed the sides of the triangles; and on being furnished with the latitude and longitude of the observatory at Land Point, computed the geodetic positions of all the points of the triangulation. In all or most of these computations he was assisted by Brevet Second Lieutenant W. P. Smith, Topographical Engineers.

Astronomical Computations.—Second Lieutenant Turnbull, Topographical Engineers, and Assistant Jas. Carr, computed all the observations for latitude made at Sand Point with the zenith telescope. Lieutenant Turnbull having been withdrawn from the survey, temporarily, the observations for longitude made at the same place on the moon and moon culminating stars were placed by me for computation in the hands of Professor George B. Bond of Cambridge observatory; and having transmitted a copy of these observations to the Bureau of Topographical Engineers, they were given for computation to professor James Major of the Washington Observatory. I take this occasion to express the indebtedness of the survey to both these distinguished gentlemen for their accurate computations. A slight difference was found in the final result as reported by each, due to the relative weight given by them to the observations made at Greenwich with the alt-azimuth instrument.

Where corrections were given for the tabulated right ascension of the moon, by both the alt-azimuth and transit-circle, Professor Bond took the mean of the two corrections; Professor Major, on the other hand, only employed the corrections as given by the alt-azimuth on those nights when the moon was not observed with the transit-circle. In addition to this cause Professor Major's result was affected by the introduction of three comparisons with corresponding observations made at the Washington Observatory. A mean of both results was taken as the longitude of the observatory. In the Appendix A will be found the report of Second Lieutenant Turnbull, giving the final result both for latitude and longitude of the observatory, which quantities are latitude 43° 54′ 49″.79 north, and longitude 5*h*. 33*m*. 22*s*.976 west of Greenwich.

It was my anxious desire in the spring, before taking the field, to obtain the longitude of the observatory at Detroit, by telegraphic connexion with some well determined observatory. The instruments, however, designed to be employed in this operation not arriving in time, the project had to be postponed to a more favorable period, which I am in hopes will be early in the coming winter.

Reduction and engraving of the final charts.

Since my last report there have been reduced and transmitted to the bureau for engraving the following charts:

One chart, part of St. Mary's river, from its head in Lake Superior to the East Neebish rapids, scale $\frac{1}{40000}$.

One chart, part of St. Mary's river, from the East Neebish rapids to Lime island, scale $\frac{1}{40000}$.

One chart, Maumee bay and river, scale $\frac{1}{30000}$.

One chart, Agate harbor, Lake Superior, scale $\frac{1}{5000}$.

These charts have been drawn and reduced in the office at Detroit by Assistant J. Mueller, assisted by Assistant P. C. Rabaut.

In addition to the charts mentioned above as completed and transmitted for engraving, Assistant Mueller has made considerable progress on the final chart of Saginaw bay, scale $\frac{1}{120000}$; and Assistant Rabaut has been engaged on the charts of Eagle river harbor and Ontonagon harbor, Lake Superior.

A list of the charts hitherto published—those now being engraved and those in course of reduction for engraving—is herewith given, that it may be compared with similar lists published from year to year.

Charts published prior to October 1, 1857.

Lake Erie, scale $\frac{1}{400000}$.
West end of Lake Erie, scale $\frac{1}{120000}$.
Kelley's and Bass islands, scale $\frac{1}{50000}$, (preliminary.)
Straits of Mackinaw, scale $\frac{1}{120000}$.
Beaver islands and north shore of Lake Michigan, scale $\frac{1}{120000}$.
Head of Green bay, scale $\frac{1}{30000}$, (preliminary.)
Sketch of East Neebish rapids, scale $\frac{1}{15000}$, (preliminary.)
St. Clair delta, scale $\frac{1}{32000}$, (preliminary.)
Buffalo harbor, scale $\frac{1}{30000}$.
Saginaw river, mouth and bar, scale $\frac{1}{10000}$, (preliminary.)

Charts published during the past year.

Harbor of Towas, scale, $\frac{1}{5000}$, (preliminary.)
Eagle harbor, Lake Superior, scale $\frac{1}{5000}$, (preliminary.)
Agate harbor, Lake Superior, scale $\frac{1}{5000}$, (preliminary.)

Charts now in the hands of the engraver.

First part of St. Mary's river, scale $\frac{1}{40000}$.
Second part of St. Mary's river, scale $\frac{1}{40000}$.
Maumee river and bay, Lake Erie, scale $\frac{1}{30000}$.

Charts now being reduced in the office.

Ontonagon harbor, Lake Superior, scale $\frac{1}{5000}$, (preliminary.)
Eagle river harbor, Lake Superior, scale $\frac{1}{5000}$, (preliminary.)
Saginaw bay, scale $\frac{1}{120000}$.
Charity islands and Wild Fowl bay, scale $\frac{1}{30000}$, (preliminary.)

Charts the data for which have been obtained in the field.

Thunder bay and Harbor of Refuge.
Harbors of Presque Isle, False Presque Isle and Middle island, Lake Huron.

Of the published charts there have been, during the past year, distributed gratuitously to owners and masters of vessels, applying at the office in Detroit, 1,675 copies of the different charts. The practice has recently been adopted, having been sanctioned by the Bureau of Topographical Engineers, of issuing the charts to the vessel or owner, and not to the master, as has been the custom previously. This practice was adopted owing to the frequent renewal of application from the same vessel for charts, on the ground of change of master. It has also been found necessary to require applicants for charts to produce the custom-house papers belonging to the vessel as evidence of its existence, there have been good reasons to believe that charts had been drawn in the name of vessels that could not afterwards be ascertained had any real existence. The demand for these charts continues very great. Daily applications are made at the office, requiring the services of one assistant to meet them, and rendering it extremely difficult to have the charts printed as rapidly as they are issued. I have, in a special report to the bureau, recommended that a nominal price be put upon these charts, just sufficient to cover the cost of paper and printing, and the experiment tried of ascertaining if, after the Government has once encountered the heavy outlay of collecting the data and engraving the chart, whether they cannot be made to pay for the printing by selling them. I am quite satisfied, from my experience, that such an arrangement would be perfectly satisfactory to those who really appreciate these charts and want them for use.

The foregoing is a succinct account of the work executed in the office during the past year. The force retained during the winter, on account of their special knowledge and services, were actively employed in repairs and alterations to the camp equipage, steamers, boats, &c., and such other matters requiring attention preparatory to resuming the field work; also in affording the usual attendance on the offices, the observatory, and as watchmen on the steamers and at the public warehouse where the property belonging to the work is stored for the winter.

Field operations of the present season.

Prior to taking the field, a project of operation was submitted to and approved by the bureau, embracing in general terms the extension of the survey of Saginaw bay, to include the whole of Lake Huron. This plan was deemed more consistent with judicious economy than to complete the survey of Saginaw bay with a portion of the force, and detach the remainder to a more distant field.

So soon as the character of the season justified, six parties were organized as follows:

Off-shore—hydrography, primary triangulations, astronomical and magnetic observations, and three for the shore-line topography and hydrography. The results produced by each of these parties, to include the 30th of September, will be briefly recapitulated in succession.

Off-shore hydrography.—This portion of the work was directed by myself, on the steamer Search. It was selected for my personal share of the work in consequence of its affording me a freer movement, thus enabling me to discharge the duties of superintendent and disbursing agent.

The steamer was placed in commission towards the close of April. The first duty performed was the search for, and discovery of, a shoal near Middle Island, Lake Erie, the existence of which had been reported to the office. The necessary examinations were made, the work connected with the survey of Lake Erie, and this shoal is now placed on the published charts of this section.

After executing the above duty, the steamer proceeded to Lake George, St. Mary's river, leaving on the way a topographical party at Thunder bay, the Department of War having placed me on Board of Engineers to examine the channels of that lake. The board were occupied several days in making the required examinations, and in drawing up the report, in which duty the steamer and party on board rendered valuable aid.

An experiment was then made to get a view over one of the lines of the large triangle projected by Capt. J. N. Macomb, Topographical Engineers, for the correction of the survey of St. Mary's river. I regret, however, to report the experiment was not successful, the flash of a heliotrope at one station not being visible from the other. After visiting Taquamenon bay, Lake Superior, to withdraw from thence some public property belonging to the survey, the steamer returned to Detroit and was occupied for some weeks placing parties in the field and erecting stations for the triangulation of Saginaw bay. Early in June the deep soundings of Saginaw bay was commenced and continued till the whole bay had been sounded. The work was also extended to the Lake Huron shores, some fifteen miles above Saginaw bay, and some forty-five miles below, as far as Forestville. Thunder bay, also, with adjacent portions of the Lake Huron coast has been sounded out.

In the Appendix B. No. 1 will be found a summary of the steamer's work. Over 1,500 square miles of hydrography have been executed, requiring 2,378 miles of lines to be sounded.

The soundings are of sufficiently minute a character to preclude the possibility of any obstacles to navigation escaping the lead. They have been carried out to an average distance from the shore of nine miles, and to an average depth of of thirty fathoms, commencing at the four fathoms curve, to which the work of the shore parties is limited. In addition to the work of sounding above reported, the steamer has been employed in transferring chronometers for differences of longitude, in visiting and moving parties, and in various other duties, requiring it to have run, as will be seen by the statement in the Appendix B. No. 1, from April 25 to September 30, over 8,000 miles in all; evidence of the active manner it has been employed. My assistants in the above duties have been for the whole time Assistant J. A. Potter, and for portions of the time Assistant D. F. Henry and O. M. Chaffe. My thanks are due to each of these gentlemen for the efficient manner they have aided me in the work.

Primary Triangulation.—This branch of the survey was placed under the charge of 2d Lieutenant O. M. Poe, Topographical Engineers, assisted by Brevet 2d Lieutenant W. P. Smith, Topographical Engineers. In order to extend the triangulation of Saginaw bay to include the line Point au Sable, Point aux Barques, it was found necessary to erect stations at each of these points, of greater altitude than had ever before been attempted on the survey—the estimated distance between these points being over twenty-seven miles. Lieutenant Poe was therefore directed to erect at Point aux Barques a station upon a plan suggested by himself, having a centre post of 100 feet in height, on which the instrument stood, surrounded by a platform for the observer—the platform being sustained by a pyramidical framework, distinct and not touching the centre post. The novelty of this design consisted in the centre post, which was composed of four sticks of timber, scarfed to make the whole length, forming a rectangular pyramid of eight feet base, and coming together at the top so as to form one post. These were braced together on the four sides by horizontal and diagonal braces, in sections arranged in such a manner that the diagonals crossed at right angles. The whole post was then additionally braced by two sets of braces, one from the ground resting against the post fifty feet from the bottom—the other resting against the post seventy-five feet from the bottom, with the feet set into the lower braces. The platform pyramid was carried up above the platform to its vertex, 36 feet in height and surmounted by a pole with a Sand's heliotrope, which stood 169 feet above the water level.

Lieutenant Poe, at Point au Sable, erected a station upon a plan devised by himself, with a centre post of 82 feet in height. The plan was similar to the one heretofore used upon the survey, except in the idea of splicing the centre post and adding a set of braces, which, putting against the top of the post, rested on the next set below.

I have been thus minute in describing these stations because I am not aware that lines of sight for a triangulation, by artificial structures of wood, have ever been secured over as great distances as we have succeeded in effecting in Saginaw bay.

Lieutenant Poe, having successfully erected both these stations, was unfortunately attacked with serious illness just as he was preparing to commence observing. The condition of his health requiring his withdrawal from active duty, I assigned Assistant James Carr to the charge of the triangulation. Assistant Carr was furnished with a 10-inch repeating theodolite, by Gambey, and a new 10-inch theodolite, by Wurdemann, both being repeating instruments and of superior character.

Owing to the difficulty experienced of obtaining satisfactory observations over lines of such great length, across water, assistant Carr was occupied during the whole balance of the season in completing the few triangles of Saginaw bay, not obtained the previous year, he having heliotropes of the most approved pattern, flashed from each station between which the angle was required. Appendix B No. 2 contains the amount of work executed by Assistant Carr to September 30. It was found impracticable to extend the triangulation beyond the line, "Point au Sable," "Point aux Barques," owing to the character of the shores of Lake Huron.

From Point aux Barques to the head of the St. Clair river the coast is comparatively straight, flat, and densely wooded, with a few scattering settlements on the immediate banks of the lake. To attempt to carry a triangulation of any proportions along this coast would have involved the cutting out of almost every line of sight throughout its whole length, and erection of stations of maximum elevations at each point. This would have required the labor of years, and consumed very nearly the whole appropriation of the survey. Such considerations, of course, precluded any such attempt. Under the circumstances it was determined to connect the survey of the shore-line by such minor triangulations as the character of the ground permitted, and to establish astronomical bases, by selecting points at convenient distances, the latitude of which should be determined with the utmost precision, and their differences of longitude with the principal meridian at Sand Point observed with all the accuracy the instruments furnished the survey rendered practicable.

In pursuance of this plan a base will be measured in the vicinity of the head of the St. Clair river, and a triangulation carried from thence up Lake Huron as far as the approachment of the Canadian shore will admit of lines of sight. An astronomical station has been established at Fort Gratiot and at Forrestville, and some intermediate point between Forrestville and Point aux Barques will also be selected hereafter. To the northward of Saginaw bay the character of the coast is more favorable.

In Thunder bar a triangulation of good proportions is attainable, which can be carried by means of Middle island as far as False Presque Isle. To connect this triangulation with that of Saginaw bay, an intermediate station has been astronomically occupied at Sturgeon Point, from which point both Point au Sable of the Saginaw triangulation and Thunder Bay island are visible. A station of maximum elevation being erected at Sturgeon Point, the azimuth from Point au Sable (25 miles distant) is obtained by direct observation, and the latitude being observed. The longitude from the principal meridian at Sand Point is deduced by computation from the data above and assumed proportions of the earth as to sphericity. In the same manner a transfer is effected to the station at Thunder Bay island, (distant from Sturgeon Point 25 miles;) and there is every reason to believe the process can be extended to Presque Isle, 30 miles beyond, and possibly to near Station Mast, the last station of the Straits of Mackinac work. As a further test, the difference of longitude between the principal meridian at Sand Point and the station at Thunder Bay island has been carefully obtained by exchange of chronometers.

The triangulation of Thunder bay has been commenced by Assistant G. W. Lamson. A base of over two miles in length, over favorable ground, has been selected and the line of sight opened. Stations had been erected at most of the points when Assistant Lamson's party was broken up, in consequence of a fewer appearing in his camp assuming an epidemic form. Assistant Lamson, however, will return to the field with another party, organized on board the steam Surveyor, and it is expected that he will complete the preliminary measurement of the base line, with the wooden rod apparatus belonging to the survey, and that he will be enabled to observe all the angles necessary to extend the triangulation above the Thunder Bay islands, connecting with Assistant Penny. The triangulation above and below Middle island has been executed by Assistant H. C. Penny, from a preliminary base measured on the main shore, abreast of Middle island.

Along that portion of the coast extending from Sturgeon Point to Thunder bay there are appearances of a broken and elevated country some distance inland, presumed to be the dividing ridges between the waters of Black, Devil, and Thunder bay rivers. This section of country is a perfect wilderness, of which little seems known, at least it has not been found practicable to obtain any definite information in regard to it. Circumstances have prevented a reconnaissance being made of this section this season, as a proper reconnaissance will, from its wild character, be the work of both time and money. It is my purpose, however, to have such an examination made as I am led to hope, from what I have seen, that there is a probability that the Saginaw triangulation by means of this elevated region, may be extended over Thunder bay, and possibly by means of elevations reported near Presque Isle, be connected with the triangulation of the Straits of Mackinaw. In the meantime, until this question can be solved, the methods above described have been resorted to, which, though wanting in the extreme precision of a great triangulation, are yet sufficiently accurate for the practical purpose of producing charts of great value to navigators, by whom they are so eagerly and unceasingly sought.

Astronomical Observations.

The foregoing account of the triangulation will afford some insight into the astronomical operations of the season. In order to carry out the plan there referred to, Lieutenant Turnbull, Topographical Engineers, assisted by Assistant James Carr, was, early in June, placed in position at Forrestville, Lake Huron.

Lieutenant Turnbull was furnished with a new transit, by Wurdeman, and a new zenith telescope, by the same maker, four sidereal chronometers and an electric clock and chronograph, made by William Bond & Sons, of Boston. It is not deemed necessary to give a minute description of the chronograph with the *spring governor*, as devised by that distinguished astronomer Professor W. C. Bond, director of the Cambridge Observatory. This will be found in detail in several scientific works, particularly in the reports of the United States Coast Survey. I feel justified, however, in bearing testimony to the simplicity and accuracy of the working of the instrument and its adaptability to field work. The clock and chronograph have this season been set apart for different stations, requiring no more care in their adjustment and handling than should be given to any instrument having pretensions to delicacy. Lieutenant Turnbull and myself, by the authority of the War Department, visited Boston early last spring to receive these instruments and be instructed in their management and use. It affords me great pleasure to take this opportunity of returning the thanks of Lieutenant Turnbull and myself to Professor Bond and his sons for their kindness and courtesy so liberally extended towards us on this occasion.

At Forestville, Lieutenant Turnbull determined the latitude by observations with the zenith telescope, and made such observations for longitude as his length of stay and the character of the weather permitted. The absolute difference of longitude between the station at Forestville and the principal meridian at Land Point was made by the careful exchange of the four chronometers twelve times between each station, the clock remaining in position at Forestville, rated by the observations there. The results of the several comparisons accorded very well with each other.

After completing the observations at Forestville, Lieutenant Turnbull was transferred to Thunder Bay island, the latitude and difference of longitude of which was determined in a manner precisely similar to the Forestville station.

Sturgeon Point, a station intermediate between Thunder Bay island and Point au Sable, was next occupied by Lieutenant Turnbull, at which position the latitude and true meridian were determined. The last point occupied by Lieutenant Turnbull is in the vicinity of Fort Gratiot, at the head of the Saint Clair river, where, it is expected, before the close of the season, he will have determined the latitude and the difference of longitude with the Forestville station. He will also make such observations on the moon and moon culminating stars for the absolute longitude of the station as the weather during his stay will permit.

The season has been, on the whole, favorable for astronomical observations, as will be seen in the abstract of Lieutent Turnbull's work, contained in the Appendix, (B, No. 3.)

In executing this duty after the withdrawal of Assistant Carr, Lieutenant Turnbull was assisted by Brevet Second Lieutenant W. P. Smith, Topographical Engineers.

Magnetic Observations.

Lieutenant Turnbull having reported that his duties as chief of the astronomical party prevented (from want of time) his making the magnetic observations, I assigned Brevet Second Lieutenant W. P. Smith to his party for the special purpose of attending to this duty. This was done prior to the transfer of Assistant Carr; afterwards Lieutenant Smith discharged the duty of assistant to the astronomical party, and at the same time observed with the magnetic instruments. These instruments were a portable declinometer, with detached theodolite for the determination of the declination and magnetic intensity—made by Jones, of London—and a dip-circle, by Barrow. Both these instruments were new, having been recently imported. The declinometer, from the delicacy of its construction and the sensitiveness of its magnets, is more calculated for a fixed observatory than for field observations. It was originally designed to furnish the party in the field with a Fox dip-circle, an instrument portable and easily manipulated, with which the magnetic elements can be readily obtained with a degree of accuracy sufficient for the purposes of the survey. Such an instrument was ordered, but had not been received on taking the field. It is intended on its arrival to confine the observations with the declinometer to the Detroit observatory, and to compare with it, before going into and on returning from the field, the Fox dip, so that the observations made with the latter instrument for the intensity, and which are only comparative, may be reduced, and the exact intensities ascertained.

The absolute magnetic elements have been obtained by Lieutenant Smith at the four astronomical stations, and it is expected he will occupy several more points before the close of the season.

I feel it due to Lieutenant Smith to bear testimony to his zeal and energy, and to the commendable perseverance with which he overcame all the difficulties of the declinometer—an instrument of not very easy manipulation to an experienced observer, and taxing exceedingly the patience. An abstract of Lieutenant Smith's work will be found in the Appendix, marked B, No. 4.

Shore-line Topography and Hydrography.

Three parties for this duty were organized early in the spring, and posted in succession on the shores of Lake Huron. The first under the charge of Assistant G. W. Lamson, having as assistants Messrs. D. F. Henry and A. Lamson, left Detroit on the 8th of May, and were placed in camp at Thunder bay. Assistant Lamson was directed to commence the survey of Thunder bay, some four miles above the light-house, and to extend his work to the south, embracing in his hydrography the four fathom curve. He was also directed to make examinations for a base line, and the projective of a scheme of triangles extending therefrom. Up to this date Assistant Lamson has executed the survey as above directed, embracing an extent of fifty-three miles of shore-line, and had selected the ground for a base, and commenced the triangulation when his party was broken up by sickness, as mentioned in a previous part of the report. Appendix B, No. 5, contains the reported details of Assistant Lamson's work for the season, which may be briefly stated as 100 square miles of topography and hydrography, and 812 miles of lines of soundings. The survey of Assistant Lamson has developed the existence of several very commodious and secure harbors of refuge in and around Thunder bay, and proves this estuary to be of much more value and importance than was before generally known. Thunder Bay river was found to have a practicable channel of seven feet of water. All these facts it is of the highest importance to make public, for though they are not claimed as discoveries, being mostly known to a few fishermen and coasters, yet the knowledge of them is confined to this limited class, whereas their publication through the charts of the survey will make them extensively known, rendering them of great value to vessels passing along the coast the main channel of communication between Buffalo and Chicago.

The second party placed in the field was under the charge of Assistant W. H. Hearding, and consisted, besides himself, of Assistants J. C. Beghein and O. N. Chaffee. Assistant Hearding was directed to resume the survey of the Lake Huron shore at the point near Point aux Barques light-house where it terminated the year previous, and to extend the same in the direction of the St. Clair river. At the present date, Assistant Hearding has reached within twenty-three miles of the river, having surveyed over fifty-one miles of the shore, and included in his work sixty-five square miles of hydrography, and twenty-eight square miles of topography. This survey includes many settlements rapidly growing into importance, such as Lexington, Bark Shanty, Forestville, &c., &c. Assistant Hearding reports many portions of this coast as steep and rocky, and in places so precipitous that no landing could be found for small boats for miles. Appendix B, No. 6, contains the general summary of Assistant Heardings's work. It is due to this party to state that Assistant O. N. Chaffee was withdrawn for one month to assist in the off-shore hydrography.

The third party in the field was placed at Presque Isle, Lake Huron, under the charge of Assistant H. C. Penny, with Assistants H. Gillman and William Casgrain. Assistant Penny commenced, about the 14th of May, the survey of the shore of Lake Huron some five miles above Presque Isle, and extended it south till he connected at Thunder bay with the work of Assistant Lamson, which junction was effected early in August. He was then transferred to the vicinity of the Sable river, and, resuming the work of 1856, extended towards the north till a junction was effected with Assistant Lamson's work at Thunder bay. This Assistant Penny has already effected, thus completing, in conjunction with the other parties, the survey of Lake Huron from above Presque Isle to within twenty-three miles of the St. Clair river. Assistant Penny measured a secondary base-line on the main shore opposite Middle island, and extended from it such triangulation as the character of the ground permitted, from Thunder bay to Presque Isle. This part of the work includes the harbors of refuge of Middle island, False Presque Isle, and Presque Isle, all of which have been minutely sounded and the data obtained for charts of the same, making public and available their capacity, channels, &c. Appendix B, No. 7, is a statement of Assistant Penny's work of the season, showing a survey of 72½ miles of shore-line, 118 square miles of hydrography, and 1,449 miles of lines sounded.

Justice to Assistant Penny requires that attention should be called to the fact, that the amount of work executed by his party largely exceeds the amounts of the other two topographical parties of equal strength with his, and no more favorably situated in regard to obstacles encountered. Assistant Penny's party, it is hoped, will be enabled before the season closes to erect the first class stations required at Sturgeon Point and Thunder Bay island.

Water level and meteorological observations.

In the last annual report, the attention of the bureau was called to the necessity of making a series of observations on the rise and fall of the water level of the several lakes; in order to ascertain, if possible, the laws of their fluctuation and their causes, it was recommended that these observations should be accompanied by meteorological observations. A special item was therefore introduced into the estimate for the pay of observers and the purchase of necessary instruments. Delay in the action of Congress on the appropriation bills induced an application to the bureau for the purchase of the instruments from the general fund for "the purchase and repair of instruments." This requisition being promptly approved, orders were immediately given for such of the required instruments as could be purchased of makers, and application made to the United States Coast Survey for permission to have constructed in that office, or under its supervision, four self-registering gauges upon the ingenious plan devised by Mr. Saxton, of that work. It affords me great pleasure to state, that this call upon the United States Coast Survey was promptly responded to with the courtesy and liberality which is characteristic of the distinguished Superintendent of this great work. Two of the gauges were made in the Office of the Coast Survey and the other two by competent mechanicians, under the supervision of that office. The meteorological instruments were ordered by James Green, of New York, whose character for excellence in this department is a guaranty of their value. The necessary time to produce these instruments after the orders were given produced so much delay that they arrived late in August. It was too late for me to visit all the points designed to be occupied to set up the instruments and instruct the observers. Operations, therefore, in this department of the survey, have this season been confined to Lake Huron, in the vicinity of the other work being carried on. Fort Gratiot, Forrestville, Point aux Barques, Towas Point, Thunder Bay islands, and Presque Isle have all had water gauges set up and observations made four times a day, which observations will be continued as long as ice is not formed. At Thunder Bay island a self-registering gauge has been set up and is in successful operation. This station has also been supplied with meteorological instruments, consisting of barometer, psychrometer, thermometer, and rain gauge. Similar instruments are furnished

Point Towas and Fort Gratiot. Great care is taken, in setting up the instruments, that they are subjected to the proper exposure, are correctly adjusted, and the observers duly instructed in their management and mode of observations. Printed forms are furnished, in which the daily observations are recorded for a month, when the results are transmitted to the office at Detroit. In the forms are columns for observations on the wind, clouds, &c., &c.

Whenever a sufficient number of observations at numerous points are accumulated, they will be placed in the hands of a distinguished meteorologist for discussion, and the production of such results as may be deducible from them.

Recapitulation of Field Operations.

From the foregoing report it will be seen that the off-shore hydrography of Saginaw bay has this season been completed, also that of Thunder bay; and in addition, a considerable portion of the off-shore hydrography of Lake Huron. That the primary triangulation of Saginaw bay has been finished, also a triangulation extended over Thunder bay, and from thence to False Presque Isle; that four points have been occupied astronomically and the dates ascertained for four astronomical bases, the latitudes and longitudes being observed at each point; that the hydrography and topography (to the four fathom curve) of the shore of Lake Huron has been executed for 177 miles of its length; in other words, the data obtained for the final charts of Saginaw bay, Thunder bay, the harbor of Presque Isle, False Presque Isle, and Middle island, and leaving but little to complete the data for the final chart of the Lake Huron coast within the limits of the United States.

Plan of Future Operations and Estimate.

In submitting an estimate to be laid before Congress, it is imperative to assume in advance the scene of future operations. It has already been reported that the survey of Lake Huron is this season nearly completed, and that it will require next season but a small portion of the existing force to bring it to a close. In any plan of future operations the completion of Lake Huron will, of course, be included. That portion of the force not required for this purpose is, however, available for another field. So far as I am informed of the wants of navigation, there are two portions of the lake region yet unsurveyed that require immediate attention. These are Lake Superior and the north end of Lake Michigan. No one can be ignorant of the importance and urgent necessity of an accurate chart of Lake Superior who is at all familiar with the increasing trade and commerce of this inland sea, or has an idea of the uncertainty and danger attending its navigation. At the same time the Fox and Manitou islands, and the navigable channels between them in the north end of Lake Michigan, should be surveyed and their dangers made known. So little is now known of this region, that only recently a notice appeared in the shipping intelligence of the public journals wherein a vessel acknowledged passing another ashore at the Fox islands with the signals of distress unrelieved, for the reason that, being ignorant of the shoals, the passing vessel was fearful of involving itself in danger. Such a confession could not be publicly made if correct charts of this region were published. I am therefore extremely anxious to extend the survey, already carried to the Beaver islands, to the Fox and Manitous, and to embrace in it a survey of Green Bay and its approaches. But in my last report I submitted an estimate containing the amount required to carry the survey on in one lake region, together with the additional sums necessary to carry it on simultaneously on other lakes. Congress was pleased to appropriate the amount designated in the estimates as necessary to carry the survey on in one lake, but at the same time required that Lake Superior should be included, the words of the act being: "For continuing the survey of the northern and northwestern lakes, including Lake Superior." I therefore consider that if a change in the scene of operations is to be made, that in view of the expression of the will of Congress, Lake Superior should be selected. The estimate is accordingly based upon this view; but as the survey of Lake Huron requires to be finished, I have estimated for a force, with equipment and supplies, sufficient for both duties. This causes the amount to be somewhat larger than the amount appropriated for the current fiscal year, but will, I trust, be granted, in view of the absolute necessity of having operations carried on in two lakes at the same time.

If it should be the pleasure of Congress to extend the survey in Lake Michigan, an appropriation of $50,000 would enable the work to be vigorously prosecuted there. As to submitting an estimate predicated on an extension of the work to proportions such as legitimately it should possess, past experience would seem to forbid. For years past the annual reports from this office have contained arguments setting forth the expediency and necessity of larger appropriations. It has been shown that true economy was promoted by liberal appropriations, and that the production of results was in a much greater ratio than the amount appropriated, due to the fact that certain necessary expenditures are common to a small and larger organization. I do not deem it necessary to burden this report with a long array of statistics of the growing commerce of the lakes and a list of disasters to vessels, with the losses of life and property consequent therefrom. These are facts which should be, and I take it for granted are, familiar to every person who studies the history and progress of the lake region. The difficulty appears to be in rendering apparent to those who are interested in the commercial prosperity of the lakes, the intimate connexion between this prosperity and correct charts. I cannot but believe, if this connexion were clearly understood, that public sentiment, expressed through the representatives and senators in Congress, would demand and receive appropriations on a much larger scale than are now or have for some time past been made. I consider my duty is confined to making known the fact, which I have done, that economy and a judicious expenditure of the public money requires larger means than have heretofore been granted. If it is the settled pollicy of the government to continue to completion the survey of the lakes, there is nothing gained by hampering its progress by inadequate means. The work is one essentially of time, and the time required is based directly upon the means furnished. There is no reason that Lake Superior and Lake Michigan should not be both surveyed at the same time, except that to do so would require, 1st, double the number of boats, persons, instruments, &c., and cost just double the amount for paying the persons and purchasing the boats, instruments, &c. The work of five years, with the existing organization, can be done in one year, with five times the means supplied as are now given, and so on. It remains for Congress alone to determine the progress of the work and the time required for its completion. I consider that I have discharged my duty when I have stated the reasons that influence me, the officer in charge of the work, to believe that the interests of the work, and through the work of the country, would be greatly advanced by the more rapid prosecution of it, and more numerous results produced were larger grants of public moneys to be made.

Very respectfully, your obedient servant,

G. G. MEADE, *Cap. Top. Engs.*

Colonel J. J. Abert,

Corps of Topographical Engineers, Washington, D. C.

APPENDIX A.

Annual Report of the Survey of the Northern and Northwestern Lakes, 1858.

Office oe the United Sates Lake Survey,
Detroit, April 17, 1858.

Sir: I have the honor to transmit herewith the accompanying papers, showing the results of the observations for latitude and longitude made at station "Sand Point," Saginaw bay, Lake Huron.

These observations were made by myself, with a twenty-six inch zenith telescope, made by Wm. Würdemann, Washington, D. C., and a thirty-two inch transit of English manufacture; no name on the telescope.

The computations for latitude were made by myself and Mr. James Carr, assistant to the astronomical party.

Table "A" shows the means of the latitude by each night's observations, the final mean, the probable error of a single observation, the probable error of the mean of the results for a single night, and the weight of the mean of each night.

The final mean 43° 54′ 39″. 79 N. which has been adopted as the latitude of the station, is deduced from the means of each night, giving to each the weight due to the number of pairs observed on and to each equal value.

The probable error of a single observation is deduced from the formula.

$$r = o.\ 845447 \frac{\Sigma\ (x - n)}{L\, m\, (m - 1)},$$

in which $\Sigma\ (x - n)$ is the sum of the differences of each observation from the mean for the night, and in the number of observations. This formula is taken from the Astromische Nachrichter.

The probable error of the mean of the results for a single night is obtained from the formula $\frac{r}{\sqrt{m}}$ r and m respecting the same quantities as in the preceding formula.

The weight of the mean of each night is obtained from the formula $W = 2 \frac{m}{\Sigma (x - n)^2}$ in which m is the number of observations, and $2\,\Sigma (x - n)^2$ is twice the sum of the squares of the differences of each observation from the mean for the night. R, the probable error of the final result, is obtained from the formula $R = \frac{\odot\ 47\ 693}{\nu\ \Sigma\ (W)}$. $\Sigma\ (W)$ equal the sum of the weights for the mean of each night.

The observations for longitude were submitted to Professors G. P. Bond and James Major for computation. Table "B" shows the results of the computations.

The differences in the results for any night arise from Professor Bond's having given equal weight to the corrections, to be applied to the tabulated A.R. of the moon, deduced from the observations with the alt-azimuth and transit-circle to reduce it to the results of actual observations at Greenwich, and interpolating for the moon's place from the quantities given in the American and British Nautical Almanacs, while Professor Major confined himself to the British Nautical Almanac and gave preference to the corrections deduced from actual observations with the transit circle at Greenwich, only using those deduced from the alt-azimuth observations on the night when no observations were made with the transit-circle; also by comparing three of the observations with corresponding ones made at Washington, which enter into his results.

I have taken the mean of Professor Bond's computations by interpolations from the American and British Nautical Almanacs as his result, and whenever Professor Major has a comparison with observations at Washington and Greenwich, the mean of the two is taken as the result of that night's observations.

The final result, 5*h*. 33*m*. 22*s*.976, or 83° 20′ 44″. 64 west from Greenwich, adopted as the longitude of station "Sand Point," is the mean of the two computations; it differs by less than 1*s*. from either, which has been considered very nearly the ultimate limit of accuracy attainable in the determination of longitude by moon culminations, though their number be increased indefinitely, and the greatest possible care is given to the computations.

The probable error of the final result ± 1*s*. 1 is deduced from the formula $r = \frac{\rho}{\nu\ n}$. in which ρ is the probable error of any one result and n the number.

Very respectfully, your obedient servant,

CHARLES N. TURNBULL,
2d Lieutenant Topographical Engineers.

GEO. G. MEADE,
Captain Topographical Engineers,
Superintendent United States Lake Survey.

TABLE A.

Latitude of the United States Lake Survey station, Sand Point, Saginaw bay.

GENERAL RESULTS.

Date.	No. of pairs observed.	Mean latitude for each night.	Probable error of a single observation.	Probable error of the mean of the results for a single night.	Weight of the mean each night.
		° ′ ″	″	″	
1857.					
July 9..........	9	43 54 40.53	0.98	0.33	0.278
11..........	10	39.67	1.49	0.47	0.114
12..........	9	39.03	0.94	0.31	0.347
13..........	10	39.22	1.89	0.59	0.069
16..........	10	39.72	1.67	0.53	0.107
24..........	14	39.70	1.55	0.41	0.089
25..........	11	39.14	1.52	0.45	0.082
26..........	10	38.99	1.62	0.51	0.093
31..........	12	39.90	1.39	0.40	0.115
Aug. 2..........	8	38.31	1.78	0.63	0.100
13..........	22	40.08	1.99	0.42	0.065
15..........	4	40.39	2.98	1.49	0.037
17..........	8	40.46	1.42	0.50	0.157
18..........	7	40.81	0.96	0.36	0.316
19..........	22	39.55	1.34	0.28	0.115
Means..........	......	43 54 39.79	1.56	0.51	ΣW=2.08

TABLE B.

Longitude of United States Lake Survey station, Sand Point, Saginaw bay.

FINAL RESULTS.

Date.	Moon's limb observed.	Resulting longitude as deduced by Prof. G. P. Bond.	Resulting longitude as deduced by Prof. James Major.	Means.
1857.		h. m. s.	h. m. s.	h. m. s.
July 2.........	I.	5 33 12.825	5 33 12.720	5 33 12.772
6.........	I.	01.455	02.390	01.992
7.........	II.	31.220	32.172	31.696
8.........	II.	24.570	24.134	24.352
9.........	II.	30.680	36.545	33.612
10.........	II.	24.660	23.526	24.093
31.........	I.	18.540	16.730	17.635
Aug. 2.........	I.	16.050	17.364	16.707
4.........	I.	25.175	26.034	25.604
5.........	II.	24.840	23.765	24.302
6.........	II.	15.135	18.743	16.939
8.........	II.	26.285	28.025	27.155
30.........	I.	11.770	15.200	13.485
31.........	I.	18.450	22.820	20.635
Sept. 1.........	I.	24.675	24.248	24.461
2.........	I.	24.055	23.370	23.712
3.........	I.	12.365	12.103	12.234
4.........	II.	43.180	46.537	44.858
5.........	II.	40.145	46.748	43.446
6.........	II.	31.785	35.106	33.445
26.........	I.	22.335	25.832	24.083
28.........	I.	23.255	*28.848	26.051
30.........	I.	22.505	*25.530	24.017
Oct. 2.........	I.	21.840	20.775	21.307
6.........	II.	20.520	*24.803	22.661
7.........	II.	10.605	12.485	11.545
8.........	II.	18.220	17.045	17.632
Means......	....	5 33 22.116	5 33 23.836	5 33 22.976

Final result Sand Point, west from Greenwich:

5h. 33*m.* 22*s.* 976=83° 20′ 44″.64—
Probable error of final result ± 1 *s.* 1.

NOTE.—The results in the column deduced by Professor G. P. Bond are the means by interpolation from the British Nautical Almanac and the American Nautical Almanac. The results marked with an asterisk are the means from comparisons with actual observations at Greenwich and Washington Observatories.

Appendix B No. 1.

Abstract of work executed by the party on board the steamer Search, during the season of 1858.

2,378 miles of deep sea soundings.
239 lines of soundings.
1,229 sextant angles for position of steamer.
3,744 readings of theodolite.
8,003 miles run by steamer on general duty other than sounding.
The necessary stations erected at different points for occupation and sounding stations.

Appendix B No. 2.

Abstract of work executed by the triangulation party in charge of Asst. James Carr, during the season of 1858.

500 square miles triangulated.
12 stations occupied.
18 triangles observed.
51 angles observed.
614 readings of theodolite.
1,343 repetitions of angles.
2,686 pointings of theodolite.

Appendix B No. 3.

Abstract of work done by the astronomical party under the charge of Lieutenant C. N. Turnbull, Topographical Engineers, during the season of 1858.

576 observations with transit on stars for time and errors of instrument.
24 observations transit of moon and moon culminating stars for longitude.
385 pairs of stars, observed with zenith telescope for latitude.
128 observations on circum-polar stars for value of micrometer.
12 transfers of four chronometers for difference of longitude.
Barometrical and meteorological observations four times daily for three and a half months.

Appendix B No. 4.

Abstract of work executed by the magnetic party in charge of Brevet Second Lieutenant W. Proctor Smith, Topographical Engineers, during the season of 1858.

2,540 vibrations of magnets.
236 angles of deflection.
280 angles of inclination.
15 angles of declination.
14 observations (half hourly) for declination.

12 observations for co-efficient of torsion,
10 observations for zero of magnet scale.
22 observations for angular value of magnet scale.

Appendix B No. 5.

Abstract of work executed by the party under the charge of Assistant G. W. Lamson during the season of 1858.

73¾ square miles of hydrography.
26 square miles of topography.
53 miles of shore-line traced.
963 lines of soundings.
812¼ miles of soundings.
30,793 casts of the lead.
4,588 theodolite pointings.
456 sextant angles.
9 observations for true meridian.
19 triangulation stations built.
101 sounding stations built.
214 buoys placed and located.

Appendix B No. 6.

Abstract of work executed by the party under the charge of Assistant W. H. Hearding during the season of 1858.

64.8 square miles hydrography surveyed.
28 square miles topography of villages and other improvements.
51⅞ miles shore-line surveyed.
918¾ miles of soundings.
996 lines of soundings.
33,089 casts of the lead.
4,652 theodolite readings.
11 sextant angles.
7 observations for true meridian.
17 light stations built.
133 sounding stations built.
185 buoys placed and located.

Appendix B No. 7.

Abstract of work executed by the party under the charge of Assistant Henry C. Penny during during the season of 1858.

118 square miles of hydrography.
20 square miles of topography.
72½ miles of shore-line traced.
1,186 lines sounded.
1,449 miles of lines sounded.
60,778 casts of the lead.
3,144 theodolite pointings.

127 sextant angles.
8 observations for true meridian.
11 triangulation stations built.
104 sounding stations built.
171 buoys placed and located.

APPENDIX C.

ANNUAL REPORT, SURVEY OF THE LAKES.

Estimate for continuing the survey of the northern and northwestern lakes, for the fiscal year ending June 30, 1858.

For a hydrographical party on steamer:

1 assistant, at $4 00 per diem, 183 days.....	$732 00	
1 assistant, at $2 50 per diem, 183 days.....	457 50	
1 sailing master, at $2 50 per diem 183 days.	457 50	
1 mate, at $1 75 per diem, 183 days........	320 25	
1 engineer, at $2 75 per diem, 183 days.....	411 75	
1 assistant engineer, at $1 50 per diem, 183 days..............................	274 50	
1 carpenter, at $1 50 per diem, 183 days....	274 50	
1 steward, at $1 25 per diem, 183 days.....	228 75	
1 cook, at $1 25 per diem, 183 days........	228 75	
1 assistant cook, at 80 cents per diem, 183 days..............................	146 40	
4 firemen, at $1 00 per diem, 183 days.....	732 00	
14 seamen, at 70 cents per diem, 183 days....	1,783 40	
Subsistence 28 men, 50 cents each per diem, 183 days..........................	2,562 00	
Fuel—600 tons of coal, at $6 00 per ton......	3,600 00	
Total for one steamer..................	12,209 30	
For two hydrographical parties, (one on each steamer)...		$24,418 60

For a triangulation party:

1 assistant, at $4 00 per diem, 183 days....	$732 00
1 assistant, at $2 50 per diem, 183 days.....	457 50
1 sailing master, at $1 50 per diem, 183 days	274 50
1 mate, at $1 25 per diem, 183 days........	228 75
1 cook, at $1 00 per diem, 183 days	183 00
1 steward, at 80 cents per diem, 183 days...	146 40
6 men, at 70 cents each per diem, 183 days..	768 60

Subsistence 12 men, 50 cents each per diem, 183 days	$1,098 00	
Hire of a vessel six months, at $200 per month	1,200 00	
Transportation of party and supplies	500 00	
Total for one party	5,588 75	
For two triangulation parties		$11,177 50

For an astronomical and magnetic party:

1 assistant, at $3 50 per diem, 183 days	$640 50	
1 assistant, at $1 50 per diem, 183 days	274 50	
1 cook, at $1 00 per diem, 183 days	183 00	
7 men, (boat's crew,) at 70 cents each, per diem, 183 days	896 00	
Subsistence 10 men, at 50 cents each per diem, 183 days	915 00	
Transportation of party and camp equipage, &c., &c	500 00	
	3,409 00	
For two astronomical and magnetic parties		6,818 00

For a topographical party, six months:

1 assistant, at $4 00 per diem, 183 days	$732 00	
1 assistant, at $3 00 per diem, 183 days	549 00	
1 assistant, at $2 00 per diem, 183 days	366 00	
1 foreman, at $1 50 per diem, 183 days	274 50	
1 cook, at $1 00 per diem, 183 days	183 00	
1 steward, at $1 00 per diem, 183 days	183 00	
2 leadsmen, at 90 cents each per diem, 183 days	329 40	
2 chainmen, at 80 cents each per diem, 183 days	342 80	
14 boatmen, at 70 cents each per diem, 183 days	1,793 40	
Subsistence 24 men, at 50 cents each per diem, 183 days	2,196 00	
Purchase of camp equipage, tools, &c., &c	250 00	
Transportation of party and supplies	250 00	
	7,399 10	
For four parties		29,596 40

Miscellaneous:

Office rent and fuel, per annum	$1,200 00	
Rent of wharf and warehouse per annum	500 00	
Pay of draughtsmen, at $4 00 per diem	1,460 00	
Pay of computer, at $4 00 per diem	780 00	
Fuel, quarters, transportation four officers	1,500 00	
Four assistants in office, at $4 00 per diem	2,912 00	
Four assistants in office, at $3 00 per diem	2,184 00	
Four assistants in office, at $2 50 per diem	1,820 00	
Steamers in ordinary	4,500 00	
Expenses in office, stationery, drawing-paper, &c., &c	500 00	
Pay of water-level and meteorological observers, 24 stations, at $10 00 per month for 12 months	2,880 00	
		$19,236 00

Contingencies:

For current expenses, such as repairs of steamers, vessels, boats; purchase of tents, cordage blocks, rigging, tools, paints, oils, &c., &c., being 10 per cent. on the whole amount	9,124 65
Total amount of estimate	$100,371 15

Respectfully submitted.

www.ingramcontent.com/pod-product-compliance
Lightning Source LLC
LaVergne TN
LVHW011141110826
845150LV00008B/2455